Whispers of Wildfire

Poetries of calm and storm

Chandni Venkatesh

BookLeaf Publishing

India | USA | UK

Whispers of Wildfire Poetries of calm and storm © 2024 Chandni Venkatesh

All rights reserved.

No part of this publication may be reproduced, stored in a retrieval system, or transmitted, in any form or by any means, electronic, mechanical, photocopying, recording, or otherwise, without the prior written permission of the presenters.

Chandni Venkatesh asserts the moral right to be identified as the author of this work.

Presentation by *BookLeaf Publishing*

Web: www.bookleafpub.com

E-mail: info@bookleafpub.com

ISBN: 9789363315525

First edition 2024

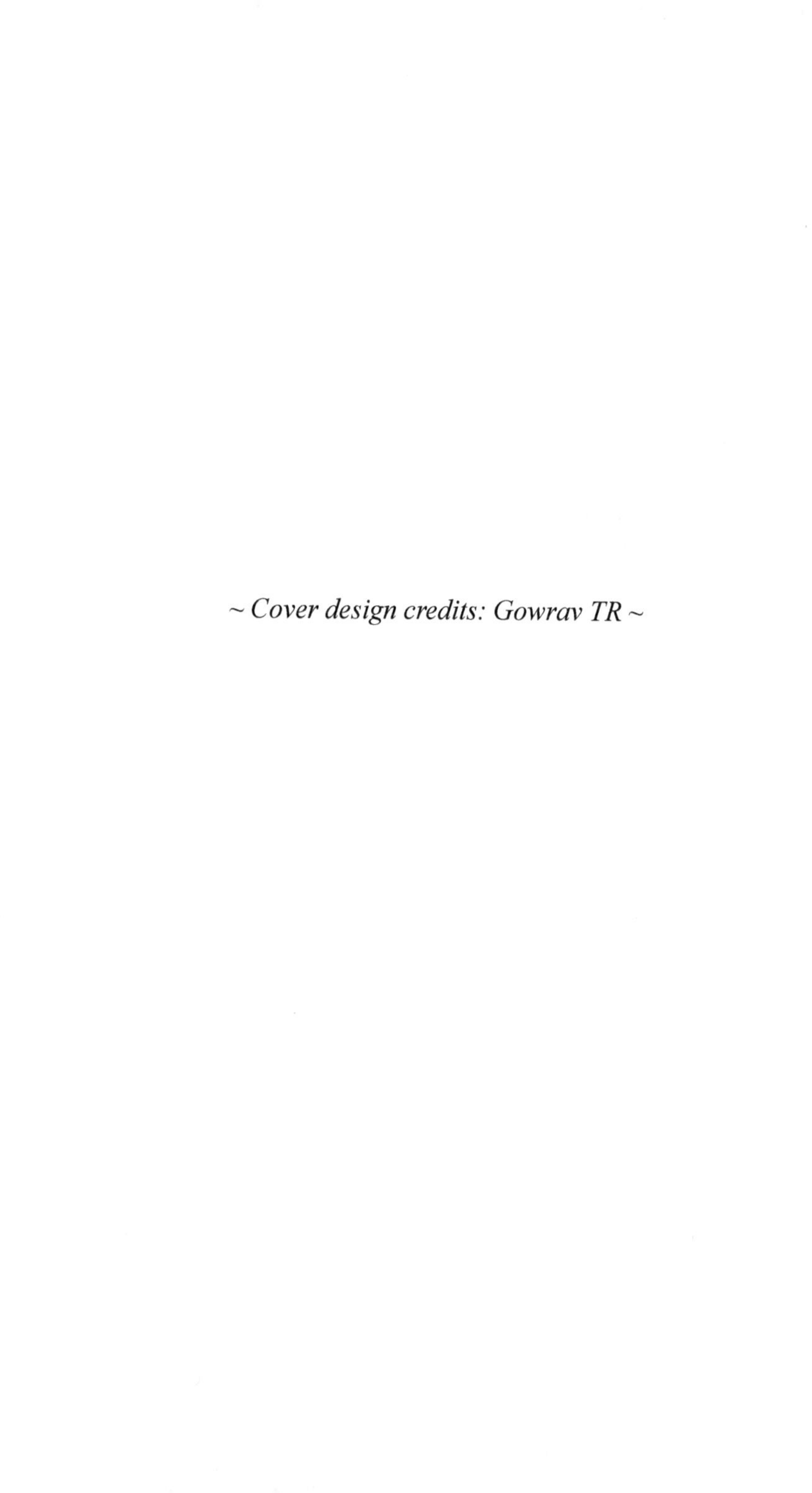

~ Cover design credits: Gowrav TR ~

To everybody who stood by my side and helped me
overcome every obstacle throughout this journey –
friends, family and *you*.

Thank you!

PREFACE

In the reposeful hours of introspection and the vibrant moments of life's tornado, poetry emerges as a faithful companion, capturing the essence of our human experience in its most raw and poignant form. This collection of poems, curated under the title 'Whispers of Wildfire Poetries of Calm and Storm,' was inspired by the fresh flowers on my table every day.

Within these pages, you will embark on a journey through the seasons of the heart, guided by the golden glow of inspiration. Each poem is a whispered promise of hope. It is a reminder that even amidst life's trails, beauty can be found. Through the prism of poetry, we discover that we are not alone in our joys or sorrows but are all interconnected on the surface of life.

May you, dear reader, see the world as I see through *'Whispers of Wildfire,'*

** ** **

Calm and storm

How is it, my dear,
That you embody both
The calm and the storm?
Your heart, a vast ocean,
Unconditional in its embrace,
Loving fiercely those who deserve it,
Yet unleashing shadows upon those you disdain.

How is it, my love,
That you carry joy
Like a secret in your pocket,
Even as you craft your quiet revenge?
You wear a brave front,
A shield against the world,
While inside, you dance with the ghosts
Of fears that whisper of loss.

My dear, before you ask,
No, you are not complicated;
You are an absolute art, woven
With threads of fire and ice,
An enigma that demands respect.
People should fear your flame,
Yet when they meet your gaze,
They find themselves drawn in,
Captivated until they melt,
Under the heat of your brilliance.

How is it, my dear,
That you walk this tightrope
Between tenderness and tempest,
A paradox that fascinates and frightens?
You laugh with the sun in your eyes,
But beneath that laughter,
A storm swirls with unspoken thoughts
And dreams that claw to break free.

How do you balance it all, my dear?
Each day, a new canvas,
Painting with both joy and sorrow,
Colours blend into a masterpiece
That few can understand,
Yet many admire from afar,
Awed by the beauty of your complexity.

So here I stand,
In awe of your fire,
Grateful to witness the storm,
To share in the calm–
A paradox of your making,
An intricate dance of heart and mind,
Forever captivated
The unique rhythm
That is entirely you.

Love, where are you?

I was waiting for
Love's call
When I chanced upon you,
I found my answer to all.
In your presence
A puzzle found its piece
A sense of completion
Contentment of peace.
Where were you lost
Through all these nights and days?
In the whispers of the wind
And the sun's subtle rays?
You may not fit the mould I had in mind,
But in your flaws, somehow,
Perfection, I find.
Your touch is the comfort
I will always crave for
Your smile, a beacon
When shadows fizzle out.
As I tie my hair in a bun
A messy-curly one
Your gaze, unwavering,
Tells tales beyond compare.
While clasping my hands
Your vows were whispered
In the rhythm of hearts

Your love silently bowed.
For each stolen kiss
While sipping coffee, I embraced
My love, I find in you
My destined place
'Oh, my heart!' I said to myself
I know you'll look for that love wherever you go
But sometimes, love is not enough
It is a fluky gift not everybody is bound for.

Imperfect love

Every imperfect turn,
Every unexpected minute,
A new face appears,
I whisper to myself,
That 'This is it; this is what I've been longing
for'
Desperately seeking
Bliss and contentment,
But the cycle repeats,
Again and again,
Until I'm shattered,
Each fracture
Adding weight to my doubt
Then, the thrill of survival points the way
Until only a shell of me is left visible
My heart was shattered
And vanished in tatters
Yet, with each break,
There is still a silver lining to the situation I'm in
I lowly defer my brokenness to the other
In a desperate bid
To be whole once again.
The jagged parts of my shattered self
Hurts everybody who glues it well
And so, the tale I tell is one of longing,
Of searching for love in all the wrong places,

A story of heartache and resilience,
In a journey called 'love'.

Whispers of love's arrival

And she'll come into your life
With a phantom of affection
Making you believe that
You've seemingly known her for years.
She will come unannounced,
Like the mist in the silent, thick, dark night
And kiss you so gentle
Like the morning dew kisses the grass.
If fortune smiles upon you,
if fate deems you worthy,
Her eyes will unveil LOVE in hues untold
Revealing its true essence,
beyond mere words,
In acts of kindness and whispers sweetly heard.
Lost in the dilemma of whether to hold her tight,
Or enjoy the tender caress of her lips
For her kiss is a revelation of long-awaited bliss,
Unforeseen, yet yearned for in every soul
Her touch is a mesmerising spell
That leaves you in awe.
Before you start wanting her all for yourself,
The dark night paved way for the sunlight
And the mist vanishes in thin air
Leaving behind the memories
Of a love that is so rare.

Shades of love

When the sky turned blue,
You stood beside me,
Sculpting the girl I knew.
To a woman so poised and remade.

When the sky deepened its colour,
Your whispers urged my independence to go
away
You taught me to stay connected, to lean on you.
To hold hands tight and never let go.

When the sky turned black to the blush of pink
We stayed close as the skies burned
Holding on to threads that stretched between us
3 AM call, long message to wake up to.
Memories!

When the heaven turned amber hue,
Our hearts knit even more tightly together,
From talks under the moonlight to dawn's soft
blow.
Dwelling in our love's warm flow.

When the sky turned crimson and dreams set
ablaze,
You chose your path and took our love along

Our dream remained unchanged deep within this
fairy's pit
Only I stood then, wearing the face of our
affection instead.

Now, the sky is screaming black,
Memories cascading down like waterfalls,
The thunderous echoes of our last love clash
I wander in tears along this lonely road of lost
love.

Longing for the day, I thought the sky would
clear,
To wash away all my sorrows
To make love reappear
To start a journey through pain.

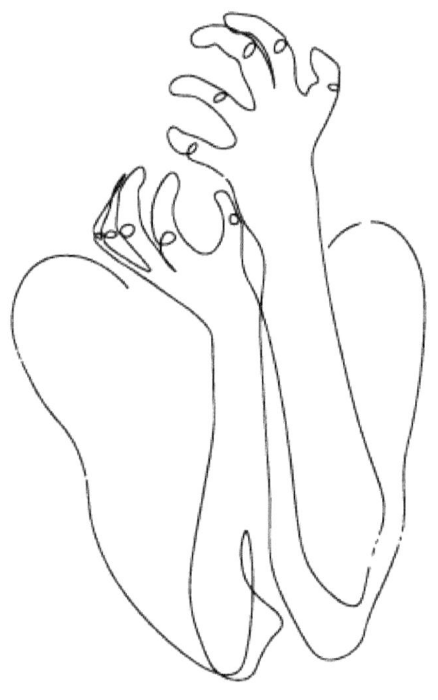

I feared

In the depths of my soul,
I trembled at the thought
That his eyes wouldn't search mine
His touch would forget my sought
And would turn cold and aloof
Leaving me deprived
A soul set adrift without a proof
I fretted. Oh, how I fretted,
That his tears might not roll down for me
His thoughts may drift away
That his love would disappear like the sea
Would his needs change?
Would his desires shift?
Leaving me alone in a world so strange
I worried, oh I worried,
He'd no longer yearn
The nape of my neck
And the warmth of my palm
I feared of him walking away
Or would he just leave
Making me question and bitterly regret
If, for once, I agreed his choice was right,
I feared of losing them all
But then, in the quiet of our shared fears,
He, too, was timorous, hiding so well.

11.11

With every second that passed,
I waited eagerly in anticipation of something
It felt like an eternity
Before the clock hit 11.11
It was our customary rendezvous
An eleventh-hour agreement
Sealed in our hearts.
We would reach out to our phones
With synchronised precision
And our voices would bridge any distance
I surmised that he would call
And so we could make a wish to the universe
That we didn't have to live miles apart.
Each wish felt like a warm connection
Wrapping around us like an embrace.
Suddenly, today, at the eleventh hour,
Time just seemed to stand still for me.
I found myself alone in a quiet room
No phone ringing broke the silence
The only sound was of my own breath
And the relentless ticking of the clock.
No impulse tingled my fingers to dial you
I waited half-expecting
A flood of emotions to gush my senses
I urged to feel the need to go back
Under the quilt where your memories

Were stuck on the fabric like glue.
In that dark moment,
I stumbled upon a revelation–
I had let you go.

Daisy

Hey there,
Today, as a way of remembering you,
I wrapped in layers of clothes
Like the colours used in summer
It was sewed in the love that never dies
And each stitch was a melody
Each curl sang their own song.
My eyes whispered secrets untold
A silent hold-on moment
I always pause, looking at you.
Sprinkled with the essence, daisy,
A fragrance so subtly loved
Yet, its sweet notes
Couldn't bridge us.
My nails painted
In the colour you once desired,
A silent plea in every stroke.
Would you look for me
Amidst the chaos
And our silent goodbyes?
In these piling memories,
I am reminiscing
Without you
I am just a shadow of your design.
Therefore, I'll tarry here,
Hoping you'd see me

And the reflection of us,
In every plea, my daisy,
I am still here
Waiting for you to recognise me.

Love's palette

Love is a vibrant palette
That blends beautifully
In the tapestry of existence
Painting life with its hues
Just as a gentle caress of a deep blue sky,
Love whispers peace
While the colour turns crimson during sunsets,
Hearts ignite with passion and desire
Love dances through the spectrum
From the soft blush of a flower
To the deep indigo at midnight,
Each of these tinges
Emerge seamlessly
On an artist's canvas,
Just like love intertwines souls.

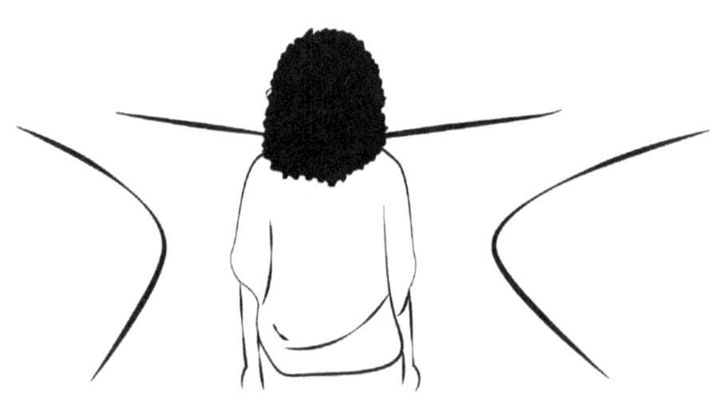

You were mine

In the quiet moments before sleep,
I didn't grasp the weight behind your plea.
'Text me when you get home,' you said,
Now I see, you were staking claim on me.
Each of our hugs lingered a little longer,
I, yet, failed to understand why you needed me
Love grew stronger with those tiny flowers
Those that you got me every time we met.
But I missed the thread that held us pledged.
Across continents, I travelled, a solitary figure in
miles,
I, yet didn't realise those missing cries.
Each compliment you bestowed, a tender plea,
Yet, I overlooked your happiness in them all.
Your words, like fragrance, adorned my days,
I failed to heed their subtle signs.
Now, walking alone in the morning's haze,
I realised it too late that,
You were always mine!

Echoes of reverie

Follow me
And I shall take you
To a place
Where the water
Whispers their secrets
Where the sun
Turns into loving fire at night
A picturesque view
As if the sky were a gold canvas
Painted in hues of fiery passion
I shall take you
Through the trees
Whose crowns are lost in the clouds
The brooks hum their own song
You know, like a symphony
In the depths of souls,
It resonates deeply.
The wind blows whistles
Its movements are so masterful
It passes a message to those who listen
And, oh, the leaves
They rustle and move
Making their own musical work
That nobody else knows.
I shall take you where you can
Throw off earthly-life shackles

Beneath the open sky
And reality's contours become blurred
Where your identity holds no power
We can sing and dance
Until we don't recognise who we are
And free ourselves.
This place is everything we cannot be
Will you come with me?

Dark romance

Beyond the feeble light around,
I see the dark romance.

I opened my eyes to a new life,
Here, your touch kept me breathing.

In the dimness where the shadows dance,
I found love that knew no bounds.

And your body odour, little like any other,
It was the fragrance that whispered.

Your eyes were like the volcano,
Drawing me deep within.

In the depths, I found love so pure,
A sanctuary where our hearts could endure.

Your touch is a gentle flame against my skin,
In it, the night grew warm, the cold dispelled.

And your luscious lips rubbed across mine,
It was as if the stars aligned.

Each kiss a spark, igniting the flame
We love and desire we couldn't tame.

Here, in the realm of our love
Is the burning kingdom of fire.

No contact

How is 'not contact' going?
I am paralysed
Without you around
I cannot feel anything else
But this emptiness inside of me.
This rage, like a storm
Has consumed whatever
Love was left of me.
Every word we spoke
Is a haunting memory
Of everything we envisioned.
Our love, once painted,
In vibrant hues of possibilities,
Are all lying shattered at my feet.
These sharp edges are cutting deep
Into the tender fabric of my heart.
Do you really think, my love,
Has all disappeared?
I cannot stop thinking about you,
Your absence is an unfillable emptiness.
I sit up and weep
Middle of the night
Dive into a whirlpool of maybes and what-ifs
With these hiccups, I grasp my breath,
The weight of your absence,
Pushes me down

Like a heavy blanket
Suffocating me in the dark.

Torch song

The man who sleeps heavy
Next to his woman,
I perceive as untouched
by a woman's gentle love.
Or perhaps that one woman in the past
turned him hopeless.
For what a woman can bestow,
There's only so much a man embraces.
For a woman's heart
Finds love when respected.
In love and affection
Not just in fleeting moments
But throughout.
Oh, let me voice for women,
'Men, you're half-loved
if you don't worship the path we walk on.
Women, grace in all we do,
Strength in our battles fought and won.
The strongest among us, I proclaim,
Are those who are wounded, still forgive,
While the pain within, a silent flame,
Burns through each beat, yet we live.
This is a torch song for the resilient,
For those who hold love's ember bright.
Let's gather courage,
In love's enduring, guiding light.

Though paths may part,
With every spark, our souls alight,
In the glow of love, we unite'.

A tale of unspoken words

Sometimes, I wonder,
How to convey my unspoken sorrow
These words, weathered by time,
May reveal the tale of our fractured tomorrow

You have left my heart in pieces,
A path filled with pain and regrets
In its midst, you discover
An almost imperceptible light

Restless nights, haunted by memories,
The ache seeps into my very being.
You were not this ideal love
But your absence is a wound never healing.

Where do we find ourselves in this wreckage,
The aftermath of our silent war?
Is it not tragic, I dare you inquire?
We are now looking through ruins, heart sore.

You chose destruction with such ease,
Yet, there was so much more you could be.
For in breaking hearts, you lost a part of
yourself,
A truth you may one day come to see.

If time permits and you dare to return,
Witness the ruins you've left in your wake.
But more profoundly, confront what you've done,
In the screams of a soul's ache.

Bound by love's flame

Our love grew,
Braided us tighter
With every moment that passed
Fondness blossoming like petals.

Somehow, amidst love,
What lingered in our minds was,
How do we navigate our paths
To cross each others'?

Every touch was a dance of passion
Setting our souls ablaze
Our kisses were intense
Igniting the flames of desire.

Craving more of your presence,
Yearning for your warmth
Wanting more of you close to me,
Lost in the spell of your affection

With the chaos of doubts
And the whispers of outside voices,
Can we stay together in this storm
Using our love as a weapon?

Each obstacle we encounter
Only serves to strengthen our connection
For true love is meant to be
Especially for you and me.

Embracing change

In the looming presence of fear
A thundering roar once terrified
But today, amidst the tempest's sound,
Change within was found

This time, tears did not flow down
Nor did the loud noise grip me
I stood firm and tall
I listened to my inner call

Not a thought was spared for what's gone
No glance back, no holding on.
I stood firm and unequivocal,
In self-assurance

In the storm's relentless spree,
I found the strength to just be me.
Though your presence may now wane,
I remain me and sane.

Regret

I left you in the eerie shade,
Chosen during the blackest hour
A sorrow that rings in the hallways of my heart
Haunted me with its incessant murmurings
By gusts of breath, I should not have ignored
Until I ran out of nothing
It took me a while
But everything became clear
It was glaringly obvious
That I was not supposed to be loved in this
manner
As the days went by,
My decision gradually solidified
A silent burden I carried,
Were tainted with the regret of leaving without a
word,
The absence of closure of a final farewell
Gnawed like a relentless predator
I watch from afar as you navigate
The labyrinth of heartache,
Your footsteps echoing
With the lessons learned too late.
It pains me to witness your suffering,
To see you grapple with the very notions of love
And respect that bound us both.
For me, the journey continues,

A path illuminated by the
Flickering flame of self-discovery.
While you remain tethered to the past,
I have forged ahead,
carving out a new beginning
From the ashes of our shared history.
And though the road ahead
Maybe fraught with uncertainty,
I take solace in the knowledge that I chose
myself,
Even as you remain trapped
In the echoes of what once was.

Strength in sorrow

As morning breaks,
My swollen eyes bear witness
To the torrents of tears shed through the night
And my limbs feel heavy with the burden of
grief.
Yet, despite the pain that threatens to consume
me,
I find the strength to rise from my bed
And face another dreadful day.
But even as I strive to move on,
I cannot shake the feeling
That while I am left to pick up
The pieces of my broken heart,
You are out there somewhere
Minding your own.
It is a thought that fills me
With bitter anguish,
And a sense of betrayal
That cuts deeper than any physical pain.
Yet, amidst the turmoil of my emotions,
There is a glimmer of hope,
A flickering flame
That refuses to be extinguished.
For I know that in time,
This pain will fade,
And I will emerge from the darkness

Stronger than before.
And when that day comes,
I will look back on this moment
Not with sorrow, but,
With gratitude for the lessons learned
And the strength gained.
So I will wipe away my tears,
Steel myself against the pain,
And take each day as it comes,
For in the end,
It is not the pain of loss that defines us,
But the courage with which we choose to face.

Oh, dear God!

Oh dear God,
The weight of my heartache
Presses down upon me,
A burden I struggle to bear alone.
I reached out to him,
Baring my soul,
Expressing the depths of my hurt,
He didn't offer any solace,
Nor did he extend
Simple courtesy of an apology.
His eyes, devoid of remorse,
Leaving me adrift
In a sea of unanswered questions.
Oh dear God,
Why did I dare to hope for more?
Was it unreasonable
For me to expect accountability,
In the wake of his actions?
Instead of healing wounds,
He caused fresh pain.
Why doesn't he love me
With the same intensity, I hold for him?
Why must he choose
To wield his words like weapons,
Imposing wounds upon my soul.
These questions plague my mind,

Tormenting me in the silence of the night
As I grapple with the painful reality
of his indifference.
Oh dear God,
Grant me the strength,
To find comfort in my own worth,
To mend the fractures of my wounded spirit,
And to forge ahead on a path
Illuminated by self-love and resilience.

The poem I left under your pillow (Part 1)

I've been with you
Those nights
I shared everything about my day
And those nights
I listened to yours
I've cried those nights
When I couldn't stomach
The fact that friends betray the worst
And those nights
When I listened to you
Complain about weather
I've been with you
Those nights when
We buried ourselves
In the moments of truth
And those nights
When we made love
And couldn't fathom, whose
Sweat was on our bodies anymore.
I've spent those rainy nights there
And I've wept a few times
Like no tomorrow
Today, I'm leaving a poem
Under this pillow
Which has witnessed most of us.

The poem I left under your pillow (Part 2)

You finally cleaned your sheets
Didn't you?
Hello there,
This verse tells you
All about us
We have struggled
To be with each other
We have loved us
Throughout.
All the ups and downs
It was not easy on
A rollercoaster ride.
Here, I'd want you to promise,
That we'd live through
Thick and thin
We do not have to just cope
With each other
But have the courage
To punch in the face
And discuss our flaws
So, my dear companion,
Be assured that our saga
Continues unabated
For as long as there

Beats a heart within
Our love shall endure
PS: I hope you've put that toilet seat down
Because baby, I'm coming home.

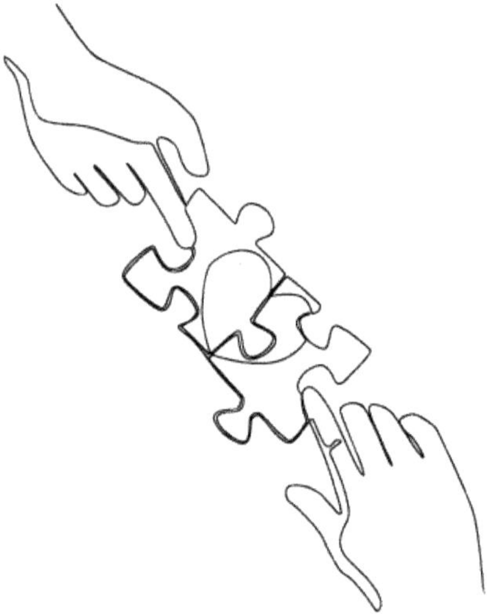

You worry me

Have you ever been so out of step,
Have I never seen you this close?
And I, find myself adrift,
Caught between the known and the unknown

Have I held your face close to mine?
In the shadows where light once danced
Your presence, once familiar and comforting,
Now trembles on the edge of uncertainty.

You trouble me in ways I cannot ignore,
For I thought I knew you as well as the back of
my palm,
Each quirk and gesture, each silent whisper,
Mapped out like the shape of my love.

But now, the lines blur, and my certainty wanes,
The face I thought I understood is now a
stranger's mask,
You worry me like a storm brewing on the
horizon,
Unpredictable and fierce in its approach.

Have I seen these signs before, buried deep,
Or did you hide them behind normalcy?
Each red flag, a shout of doubt I missed,

Or perhaps, they emerged where once they were
concealed.

In every corner of my mind, I search for clarity,
Yet the more I seek, the more elusive you
become.
You trouble me with every breath and every
silence,
A puzzle I cannot piece together, a mystery
unfolding.

So here I stand, grappling with my own
confusion,
As the familiar becomes strange and the known
becomes hazy.
You worry me more than you could ever fathom,
As I navigate this new, unsettling path, you
worry me!

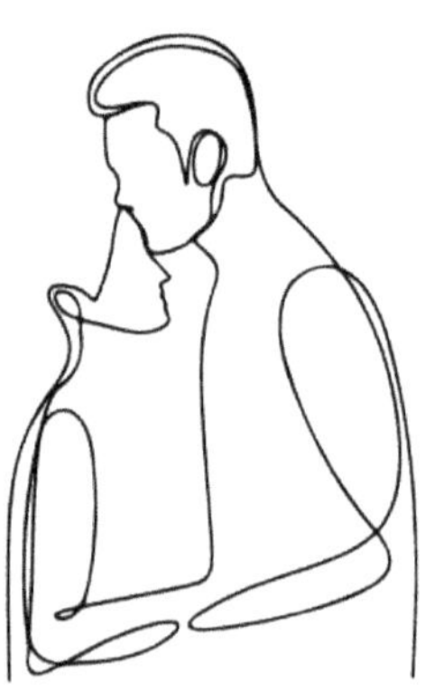

Off guard

How was it, you asked?
Have you ever truly known
What it feels like to gasp for breath,
To be caught in the brief pause
Between longing and fulfilment?
Have you felt the 'oh my god' moment?

What caught me off guard
Was how, when we kissed,
It defied all expectations
It wasn't awkward or misplaced.
No, it was deeply reassuring,
A profound comfort,
Wrapped in a sense of being cherished.

When you took my chin in your hand,
And held me close around the waist,
I found myself wishing
For time to come to a halt,
Forever to be in that feeling.

Do you remember,
How you touched me with tenderness?
That made me feel like I was wholly yours.
You brushed the hair from my face,
And each gentle gesture was a hug of affection.

Did you, too, experience those butterflies,
Fluttering wildly as I rested on your shoulder?
It felt like home in the purest sense,
And your hugs,
They carried a palpable energy,
A warmth that spoke volumes without words.

You treated my lips as though they were
The sweetest, most treasured fruit,
And that moment when you kissed my neck
Why, oh why?
Every part of that experience was intoxicating,
And I find myself reliving it
With every passing minute now.

Love I found vs. love that found me

You were the love I didn't know I was missing,
A presence that arrived like a sudden storm,
Transforming my calm waters into a turbulent
sea.
In that chaos, I questioned if serenity was what I
truly needed,
Embracing the tempest as if it were my heart's
only beat.
The whirlwind of emotion felt like a revelation,
A truth I believed was love's pure form.

Now I see with clearer eyes,
You are the love I truly need,
A steady force, quietly weaving into my
existence,
Without fanfare or frenzied entrance.
In my search for excitement,
I mistook turbulence for connection,
Settling for the chaos that only masked the void.

You've gently illuminated what I truly crave–
A love that builds, not one that shatters.
You've shown me the difference
Between fleeting thrill and lasting depth.

In you, I've found a partner who battles demons
Without becoming one.

Where were you in the chapters I wandered
alone?
Why did our paths not cross sooner?
The answer remains elusive,
But now, I cherish the journey that led me to
you.

What if I were wrong?

What if I were wrong
About everything I've come to know?
About the way I love,
The way I harbour resentment?

What if I were mistaken
In my perceptions,
The thoughts I hold dear,
The very essence of this life I live?

What if I misjudged
The intricacies of people,
The depths of your soul?
Or if my understanding of it all
Is merely a fragile illusion,
A tapestry woven from threads of doubt?

What if the truths I cling to
Are nothing more than shadows,
Distorted reflections in a mirror
That shows me only what I wish to see?

What if my heart,
With its fervent hopes and fears,
Is leading me astray,
Casting me into a labyrinth
Of uncertainty and confusion?

What if I am wrong
About the world,
About love and hate,
About the connections we forge?

In this vast expanse of existence,
Could it be that my certainty
Is merely a flickering candle
In the face of an overwhelming darkness?

What if, in my quest for understanding,
I've overlooked the beauty
Of uncertainty itself,
The grace of simply being,
And the possibility that perhaps,
Not knowing might be the key
To truly connect with you
And the world around me?

Hi, you

What is it in you
That sets you apart,
That draws people in
Like moths to a flame?

What is it in you
That ignites such fascination,
That makes hearts race
And thoughts linger long after you're gone?

Is it the way your eyes
Hold a thousand stories,
Sparkling with a light
That seems to understand.
Or perhaps it's your laughter,
A melody that dances through the air,
Infusing every moment with joy,
Turning the mundane into magic.

Is it the warmth of your conversation,
The way you make everyone feel seen,
Or the effortless charm
That wraps around you like a favourite blanket?

What is it in you
That captivates so effortlessly,

That leaves a lasting imprint
On the souls you encounter?
Why do people find it hard
To let go once they've met you,
As if a piece of their heart
Has become entwined with yours?

Is it your authenticity,
The way you embrace the world
With open arms and a tender spirit?
Or is it the mystery that surrounds you,
The layers waiting to be discovered,
Inviting others to delve deeper
Into who you truly are?

What is it in you
That lingers in memories,
That becomes a part of dreams,
A beautiful enigma
That calls to be understood?

In a world filled with fleeting moments,
You are a presence that remains,
An echo of something profound,
And I can't help but wonder–
What is it in you
That makes you so irresistibly special?

The night we met

Take me back
To that night,
When I lingered in anticipation,
Eager to meet you,
To that night
When our paths had just crossed,
And I hadn't known
The warmth of your hands,
Or felt the comfort of leaning
Against your shoulder.

Take me back
On the moment
When uncertainty lingered
In the air,
When I didn't know
If I should pull you close
Or admire you from a distance,
To that magical night
When our eyes first met
And a spark ignited,
Filling the space between us
With unspoken promises.

Take me back
To the delicate dance

Of our laughter,
When my smile lit up your world
And your joy made me spin,
When innocence enveloped us,
And love was a secret
Whispered softly over dinner,
When we sat together
With crumbs of joy
On my lips,
And you leaned in,
Gently asking,
'Hey! Do you mind'?

Take me back
To that night,
When we were unaware
Of the chaos that awaited,
When your eyes sparkled with hope,
Yet shimmered with the hint
Of tears as I prepared to leave.
We were just two souls,
Unravelled and free,
Embracing a moment
That felt like an eternity.

Take me back
To that night,
Before we learned the weight
Of what it means to love,

When every glance held the thrill
Of possibility,
And every heartbeat was a step
Into the unknown.

Take me back
To the night we met,
Before the world shifted,
When everything felt right,
Before the chaos unfolded,
When we were simply
Two hearts on the brink
Of something beautiful.

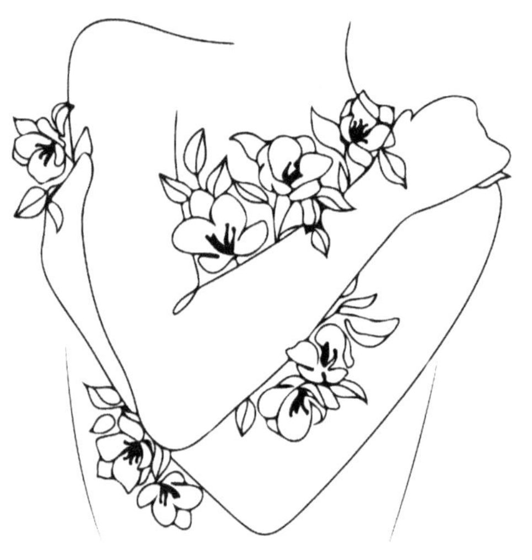

What I mean by love

When you say you love me,
I have always asked you why.
It is not enough that you say,
You love me for my curly hair,
My voice, my laughter or my very existence.
'Coz that feels like saying,
'I love the flower-filled trees,
The sun, when it's almost setting,
The clouds, when they're heavy,
The rain when it's drizzling.'

Do you see what I mean?
Your love feels conditional.
True love, I believe,
Means to embrace the trees when they stand
bare,
To cherish the sun from dawn till dusk,
To admire the clouds in all their moods
Blue, grey, gold and the deepening hues.
To love the rain when it pours,
As if the sky itself has torn.

I yearn for a love that reaches deep,
That sees me in every season,
In every shade of my being.
Love that cherishes for not just who I am now,

But who I have been and who I will become.
To find beauty in my flaws,
To hold me close when the world feels cold.
Can you see me in those moments?
When I am lost, when I am vulnerable,
When the light dims, and shadows grow

Love, I wish, should be a vast ocean,
Endless and unyielding,
An embrace that withstands the storms,
That sees beauty in the unadorned.
So tell me, can you love me like that?
Not just for my laughter but for my tears,
Not just for my strength, but for my fears?
I want to be loved wholly,
For my past, the present and the future